THE HOLOCAUST

THE FACES OF RESISTANCE

Stuart A. Kallen

Published by Abdo & Daughters, 4940 Viking Drive, Suite 622, Edina, Minnesota 55435.

Library bound edition distributed by Rockbottom Books, Pentagon Tower, P.O. Box 36036, Minneapolis, Minnesota 55435.

Printed in the United States.

Cover Photo credit: Bettmann Archive
Interior Photo credits: Bettmann Archive, pages 6, 8, 9, 14, 15, 20, 31, 33
                        Archive photos, pages 26, 38
                        Wide World photos, page 29
                        Sygma, pages 35, 43

Edited by Rosemary Wallner

Library of Congress Cataloging-in-Publication Data

Kallen, Stuart A., 1955-
    The Faces of Resistance / Stuart A. Kallen.
        p.   cm. -- (The Holocaust)
    Includes bibliographical references and index.
    ISBN 1-56239-353-7
    1. Holocaust, Jewish (1939-1945)--Juvenile literature. 2. World War,
    1939-1945--Jews--Rescue--Juvenile literature. [1. Holocaust,
    Jewish (1939-1945) 2. World War, 1939-1945 -- Jews -- Rescue.
    3. Righteous Gentiles in the Holocaust.] I. Title. II. Series:
    Holocaust (Edina, Minn.)
    D804.3.K34   1994
    362.87'089'92404--dc20   94-25727
                                                        CIP
                                                        AC

Table of Contents

FOREWORD

The Holocaust is a tragic time in world history. It was a time of prejudice and bias turned to hate and the persecution of an ethnic group by persons who came into a position of power, allowing them to carry out that hate.

The Holocaust series depicts what prejudice and biases can lead to; how men, women and children—simply because they were Jewish—died horrible deaths.

When a child is born it has no prejudices. Bias must be learned and someone has to display it.

The goal of this series is to enlighten children and help them recognize the ignorance of prejudice so that future generations will be tolerant, understanding, compassionate, and free of prejudice.

Acknowledgments:

Rabbi Morris Allen
        Beth Jacob Congregation

Dr. Stewart Ross
        Mankato State University

Special Thanks to The United States Holocaust Memorial Museum

CHAPTER ONE

THE FINAL SOLUTION

*I*n 1933 Adolf Hitler and his political party, the Nazis, seized the reigns of power in Germany. Immediately, the Nazis passed a series of laws to deny civil rights to all Jewish people. The Nazis took all property away from Jewish people. They burned Jewish temples. The Nazis fired Jews from their jobs. They beat and humiliated Jewish people in the streets. They built huge prison camps, called concentration camps. By 1945, the Nazis had built 9,000 camps. The Nazis rounded up Jewish people and sent them to the camps.

By 1940 Hitler and the Nazis had total control of most of Europe. From Spain to the Soviet Union, from Greece to Finland, the Nazis hunted down Jewish men, women, and children and murdered them. They sent some to death camps, they killed others where they lived. Thousands of railroad trains pulling cattle cars packed with Jews rolled into the death camps day after day.

By 1942 Hitler and his followers had put into place the plan to exterminate every single Jewish man, woman, and child. The Nazis called this plan the "Final Solution." Six major death camps and dozens of small ones began the industrial task of reducing millions of people to ashes.

At the camps, Nazi guards stripped Jewish people and sent them to gas chambers that were disguised as showers. After they were dead, prisoners shaved their heads and used the hair to make clothing for German soldiers. They took gold teeth from the corpses and melted them down into gold ingots. They burned the bodies in ovens called crematoria. Millions upon millions died this way. During the summer of 1944, the Nazis killed up to ten thousand Jews *a day* in this manner.

By the time the Nazis had finished their work, 4,500 Jewish towns in twenty countries were wiped off the map. Over six million Jews were dead.

Nazi troops clean out this ghetto in Warsaw, Poland.

CHAPTER TWO

THE COLLABORATORS

*T*he Nazis, however, did not act alone. All across Europe, the process of finding, rounding up, transporting and murdering Jewish people depended on the help of local Nazi supporters, called collaborators. In some places, especially Eastern Europe, when locals heard the Nazis had invaded, they killed their neighboring Jews before the Nazis could get there.

Many times, when Jews went into hiding, collaborators turned them in for a small reward. Jews who were not turned in were often blackmailed. They were forced to provide money, or even slave labor, to buy the silence of their neighbors.

Many people simply shrugged their shoulders and turned away when they saw the Nazis rounding up the Jews. Those who remained neutral aided the Nazis with their inaction.

The powerful Roman Catholic church did not speak out against Nazi killing. In cities, towns, and villages, tens of thousands of priests saw Nazis empty houses, and wipe entire villages off the map. They heard the confessions of the killers. In 1942 the Vatican's own diplomats delivered accurate information about the mass murders to the Vatican. Yet the official silence hung like a cloud over the Nazi atrocities.

Some nations, including the United States, remained "neutral" to the matter of the mass murder.

In nations where hatred of the Jews, or anti-Semitism, was widespread, the Nazis had no problem putting their Final Solution into place. In Latvia, Lithuania, and Poland, nine out of ten Jews were killed with the help of collaborators. In Denmark, where anti-Semitism was not taught, nine out of ten Jews were saved.

*Nazi troops march into the Warsaw
ghetto after bombing and shelling.*

CHAPTER THREE

THE RESCUERS

Whosoever preserves one life is as though he has preserved the entire world. — The Talmud, the Jewish book of laws.

*T*he majority of Europeans ignored the Holocaust. Yet there were uncounted thousands who risked their own lives to help the Jews. Some were single individuals. Some worked in groups. Entire towns sheltered the Jews in their midst. In Denmark almost everyone rallied to stop the Nazis from deporting the Jewish citizens to the death camps.

The motives of the rescuers differed from one person to another. Some were tied to Jews by friendship, family, or marriage. Some simply helped total strangers out of a moral desire to fight evil. Some were driven by political, ethical, or religious beliefs. Many of the rescuers felt that they

Elie Wiesel, Holocaust survivor.

were acting out of simple human decency. Later, after the war, people around the world called these rescuers heroes. But they didn't feel that they were heroes. They were just doing what any human being should do to help another who is in danger. As Holocaust survivor Elie Wiesel said: "In those times, one climbed to the summit of humanity by simply remaining human."

CHAPTER FOUR

THE RESCUERS OF DENMARK

*O*f all the Nazi-occupied countries, Denmark stands out as the only nation that rescued almost all of its Jewish citizens. The country had a long tradition of tolerance and acceptance of Jews. The people of Denmark did not consider Jews to be outsiders, but as Danish citizens with equal rights.

In 1940 the Nazis invaded Denmark. But the Germans looked at the Danes as friends. The two countries had a similar language and the Nazis let the Danes run their own country. The Jews were left alone.

By 1943, however, Danish Jews were no longer immune from the Final Solution. Plans for the deportation of Jews was leaked to the Danish government. On September 17, 1943, the Nazis seized a list with the names of all the Jews. On September 28, a German naval attaché alerted the Danish government that the Nazis were about to round up the Jews and deport them.

Danish response was immediate. Farmers, businesspeople, homemakers, taxi drivers, doctors, fishermen, and the clergy joined forces to save the Jewish people. Those who had been peacefully resisting the Nazis jumped at a plan that would save lives without firing any shots.

On the eve of the Jewish New Year, Jews canceled their religious services. Rabbis instructed the Jews to go into hiding. Jews left Copenhagen and other cities by train, car, taxi, and on foot. They found hiding places in hospitals, churches, homes, and farms. Some Danes formed a plan to evacuate the Jews by sea.

The Lutheran Bishop to Copenhagen urged Danes to save the Jews.

He said:

> "We shall fight for the cause that our Jewish brothers and sisters may preserve the same freedom which we ourselves evaluate more highly than life....We must obey God before we obey man."

Money was raised to rent fishing boats. Some Jews were able to pay for the boats themselves. The Jewish community obtained a loan using their possessions as a guarantee. (This loan was repaid after the war.) Churches, and even total strangers, helped those who could not afford passage.

A total of $650,000 was raised to rescue the Jews. Scores of Danish fishermen risked their lives—the penalty for helping the Jews was death.

During October 1943, 7,220 Jews left Denmark on fishing boats. Danish police came to the aid of the rescuers. Coast guard vessels lent support. For two weeks, the narrow strait that separated Denmark from Sweden was afloat with boats spiriting Jews to safety.

Sweden was not occupied by the Nazis. And that country provided a safe haven for the rescued Jews. This was in spite of the fact that the Nazis would consider such action an act of war. But by 1943, the Nazi Army was on the run from Africa to the Soviet Union. It was only a matter of time before the Allies defeated them.

The only Jews who could not escape were old people and people with disabilities. Medical care simply could not be provided to those who could not walk or run from the Nazis. Still, "only" 464 Jews fell into Nazi hands after the rescue.

Historians wonder what separated Denmark from the rest of the European countries. For one thing, there were only 7,500 Jews in Denmark—a small amount. And the King of Denmark, Christian X, spoke out publicly against the deportation. Most Danes simply felt that when an enemy occupies your country, you do not aid them in their wrongdoing.

In addition, even the Nazis treated the Danes with respect. They left the Danes' democratic government in place. This allowed an organized effort through public channels to save the Jews. No other Nazi-occupied country had this luxury.

The rescue involved more than people. The Danes carefully protected Jewish property. The recorded valuables and placed businesses in trust. They stored sacred Jewish religious objects, such as Torah scrolls, in churches and returned them to the Jews after the war.

The Danish government was also very concerned about its Jewish citizens who fell into Nazi hands. The Danish Jews were sent to a "model" concentration camp called Theresienstadt. This camp was a sham. The Nazis showed it to the world in a propaganda effort to hide the true horrors of the real death camps. The Red Cross was even allowed to visit the camp in 1944. Although it was a hoax, the Danish Jews who lived there fared much, much better than the Jews in other places.

The Danish Jews who went to Theresienstadt were the first to be released. They returned home days after the war ended. Of the 464 Jews deported, only fifty-one died.

CHAPTER FIVE

THE FRENCH RESCUERS

*N*o other government of any country cooperated more with Nazi policies than France. The French wrote their own anti-Semitic laws before the Nazis urged them to do so. They used French police to hunt down Jews, and voluntarily deported Jews from the southern regions not occupied by the Nazis. In other Nazi-occupied territories, a person faced persecution and death if they had three Jewish grandparents. Under French law, a person need have only two Jewish grandparents.

Though the government cooperated, common people in France provided a huge resistance to the Nazis. In the summer of 1942, the Nazis began forceful deportation of Jews to concentration camps. A pastor from the city of Toulouse wrote a letter that read:

> "Why does the right of sanctuary no longer exist in our churches? The Jews are real men and women. Not everything is permitted against these men and women; against these fathers and mothers. They are part of the human species. They are our brothers and sisters, like so many others."

This letter spread like wildfire throughout southern France. Many priests read it to their congregations. People carried it hand to hand and sold it in Catholic bookstores. Soon a few Catholic priests began hiding Jewish children. The clergy used the Church's access to birth certificates and baptismal papers to forge documents for Jews in hiding.

With papers showing them to be Catholic, many Jews were able to escape to neutral Switzerland. All together, the French hid about 7,000 Jewish children in private homes and religious institutions. Those who did not help mostly remained silent about Jews hiding in their midst. In that way, the Nazis were again foiled.

The Quakers, YMCA, and Swiss Red Cross were other groups that helped French Jews.

Because of help from average French men and women from all walks of life, 200,000 of France's 300,000 Jews were saved from death at the hands of the Nazis.

The French Resistance fights a pitched battle against the Nazis in the streets of Paris, France, 1944.

*Clad in an outfit designed for action, this young French girl keeps close
to a wall and holds her submachine gun ready to fight at a moment's
notice. She is part of a patrol assigned to rout German snipers still
hiding out in Paris, 1944.*

CHAPTER SIX

REFUGE IN A MOUNTAIN VILLAGE

*I*n southern France, not far from Lyon, there is a village named Le Chambon-sur-Lignon. During the Holocaust years, most of the people in the village were French Protestants who were called Huguenots. The Roman Catholic majority in France had persecuted the Huguenots for three hundred years. They were keenly aware of their position as outsiders in French society.

When the Nazis invaded France in 1940, they only ruled Northern France. Le Chambon was ruled by a Nazi-controlled French government called the Vichy government. In 1942 the Nazis took over the entire government of France.

The Protestant pastor of Le Chambon was André Trocmé. With the help of his wife, Magda, Trocmé oversaw vast operations sheltering thousands of Jewish refugees in the mountainous village. Other Protestant organizations and many Catholic clergy helped the Trocmés.

By their words and actions, the Trocmés put their lives, as well as the lives of their children, in jeopardy.

Resistance to the Nazis started with a few small gestures. Trocmé and the villagers refused to salute the Vichy flag. They also refused to sign loyalty oaths to the leader of the Vichy government. Vichy soldiers silenced the church's bells.

These actions inspired the young people of Le Chambon to get involved. When the Nazis deported Jews from Paris, students wrote a letter of protest to a visiting official.

Magda Trocmé was the grand organizer of the operation where people housed Jewish adults and children in public buildings and children's homes. Some stayed with local villagers in their homes. With guides, some were taken on the dangerous trek to the Swiss border. Most of the refugees had come from Germany and barely spoke a word of French.

The Swiss police were against anyone smuggling Jews into their country, and could not be trusted. Once in Switzerland, the Huguenots handed over Jewish refugees to other Protestant volunteers.

Trocmé's cousin Daniel ran a children's home almost totally composed of Jewish children. A German army chaplain found out about the home and reported it to the Nazis. Daniel was arrested and sent to Buchenwald death camp where he died in 1944. He told the Germans, "I defend the weak."

At one point the Nazis asked Pastor André Trocmé for a list of Jews who were living in his town under false names. Trocmé replied, "Even if I had such a list I would not pass it on to you. These people have come here seeking aid and protection....I don't know what a Jew is, I only know human beings."

The full story of Le Chambon will never be known. After the war the villagers were humble about their life-saving actions. Like many other rescuers, they did not think that they were heroes. One said:

> "Things had to be done, that's all, and we happened to be there to do them. Helping these people was the most natural thing in the world....Well maybe it was unreasonable. But you know, I had to do it anyway."

CHAPTER SEVEN

THE BELGIAN RESCUERS

Germany invaded and conquered Belgium in May 1940. The Belgian Army laid down its arms, and the government moved to London, England. During World War I, the German Army had been unbelievably cruel to Belgium. This time they decided on a less harsh occupation. The Nazis allowed the country to govern itself, using the laws already in place.

When the Germans tried to force their anti-Semitic policies on Belgium, government authorities protested loudly. Mayors, professors, and priests joined in the chorus of outrage. As early as 1940, there was a coordinated Belgian effort to frustrate the Nazis.

Many of the 90,000 Jews living in Belgium fled to France when the Nazis arrived. Some 60,000 remained. When the Final Solution went into high gear in 1942, 30,000 Belgian Jews were sent to death camps. The other 30,000 were saved.

As in France, the Catholic church helped whomever they could. Jews were given false papers and hidden in church institutions. Father Bruno from Louvain rescued over 300 Jewish children by pleading with families to accept these frightened children. This was while the Gestapo was on Father Bruno's trail.

Compared with other countries, Belgium stood out for its display of secular and religious leadership during the Holocaust.

CHAPTER EIGHT

100,000 SAVED BY RAOUL WALLENBERG

*T*he country of Hungary was an ally of Nazi Germany. But the Jews there remained relatively untouched until the middle of 1944. By then the Nazis knew that they were going to be defeated. But even this did not prevent the Nazis from carrying out the Final Solution against the Hungarian Jews. They knew perfectly well the war was lost when they began to murder these Jews.

Furthermore, the Nazis could not carry out the deportations in secrecy—as they had from 1942-1944. By 1944 the United States, Britain, the Soviet Union, and the Vatican had firsthand knowledge of the death camps. The Nazis killed Hungary's Jews openly, in the full view of the world.

Hungary controlled territory that held 725,000 Jews. Between May 14 and July 8, 437,402 of those people were gassed at Auschwitz. It took 148 trains to carry them to the camps. On some days 10,000 Jews died. The deportations were suspended in the face of the advancing Soviet Army. By then only 200,000 Jews remained, most of them in Budapest.

In January 1944, U. S. President Franklin D. Roosevelt established the War Refugee Board. The War Refugee Board's main function was to rescue the Jews of Hungary. They asked for help from the Vatican, Switzerland, Sweden, and the Red Cross. Sweden was the only one that answered the call.

Raoul Wallenberg, secretary to the Swedish legation in Budapest during World War II. He was taken prisoner by the Russians in 1945. The Soviets have now declared that Wallenberg died in a Moscow prison in 1947.

Raoul Wallenberg was chosen to lead the rescue operation. He was a Swedish aristocrat, the heir of a respected banking family. He was also an architect who had been schooled in the United States. Wallenberg knew Jews from his work as a banker.

Wallenberg was given a diplomatic passport, a huge sum of money, and permission to use any methods possible to rescue the Jews. He arrived in Budapest on July 9, 1944. By then the deportations had been halted. Wallenberg began issuing fancy passports bearing the Swedish seal. Five thousand of these were quickly snapped up. With official passports, Jews could leave Hungary.

The government of Hungary and some Nazi officials knew they were doomed to lose the war. They were extending hands of peace to the Allies in hopes of saving their own necks. They looked the other way as Wallenberg continued his activities.

Wallenberg set up hospitals, nurseries, and soup kitchens for the Jews of Budapest.

In November the Nazis began a series of forced death marches. They marched all Jewish men between the ages of sixteen and sixty to the Austrian border without food, water, or warm clothing. Those that could not walk were killed. Thousands died.

Wallenberg acted quickly. He issued thousands of Swedish safe passes. He pursued convoys carrying Jews. He roamed through the streets harassing German and Hungarian officials to release Jews in their custody.

When threats did not work, Wallenberg offered bribes. He even stood between Jews and their captors and said they would have to take him first. He forged papers and driver's licenses. His air of authority even scared the Nazis. Adolf Eichmann, the man in charge of the Final Solution, threatened Wallenberg with death. Still, Wallenberg would not back down.

When the Soviet Army entered Budapest on January 16, 1945, 100,000 Jews were still alive. Most of them owed their lives to Wallenberg and his helpers. Through his heroic deeds, Wallenberg had saved them.

At that point, Wallenberg should have been making plans to return home. Instead he approached Soviet officials with his plans for the Jews in post-war Hungary. On January 17, Wallenberg was seen in the company of Soviet soldiers. He said, "I do not know if I am a guest of the Soviets or their prisoner." He was their prisoner. Wallenberg was never seen as a free man again.

For ten years the Soviets denied Wallenberg was their prisoner. In 1956 the Soviets produced a death certificate for him saying he had died of a heart attack in 1947. Yet there were reports of an aging Swedish man in Soviet prison camps until the 1980s. In 1991 Soviet leader Mikhail Gorbachev returned Wallenberg's passport to his family. To this day, no one knows the ultimate fate of Raoul Wallenberg, the man who saved 100,000 Hungarian Jews.

CHAPTER NINE

THE JEWS OF BULGARIA

*B*ulgaria joined forces with Nazi Germany in 1941 to gain territory. After helping attack Yugoslavia and Greece, Bulgaria was able to acquire the areas of Macedonia and Thrace. Bulgaria's pro-Nazi leader passed legislation to restrict Jewish rights.

Unlike many European countries, there was not much anti-Semitism in Bulgaria before the war. When the anti-Jewish laws were passed, there was an uproar from writers, doctors, lawyers, political leaders, and the Holy Synod of the Bulgarian Eastern Orthodox Church. Farmers threatened to lie on the train tracks that would carry the Jews away.

When the Nazis pressed Bulgaria to deport the Jews in 1943, a secret agreement was reached. The Bulgarians said that the Nazis could take the Jews of Macedonia and Thrace. Later, the Bulgarians promised, the Nazis could deport Bulgarian Jews. In March 1943, 12,000 Jews were taken from Macedonia, Thrace, and eastern Serbia. They were murdered at Treblinka death camp.

Still, the attempt to deport Bulgarian Jews met with stiff resistance. Even the Jewish community there was bold enough to hold public protests against the Nazis. But Jewish persecution got worse. The Jews of Sophia were driven out of the city. Jewish men between the ages of twenty and sixty were sent to slave labor camps.

Because of the actions of the Bulgarian king, church, and common people, 50,000 Bulgarian Jews survived.

CHAPTER TEN

JEWS IN ITALY

*J*ews had moved into Italy before the birth of Christ. They had lived there hundreds of years before St. Peter, the first bishop of Rome. By the time of the Holocaust, one out of every one thousand people in Italy (one-tenth of 1 percent) was Jewish. Most of the 47,000 Italian Jews were treated equally in Italian culture and society. In 1920 the president of Italy's highest court was Jewish. In the 1930s, eight percent of all Italian professors were Jewish.

Benito Mussolini was the ruler of Italy before and during World War II. Mussolini was Hitler's ally and Italy and Germany fought the war together. But as long as Mussolini remained in power, no Jews were deported from Italy or Italian-controlled territories. The Nazis took control of Italy in 1943 and tried to carry out the Final Solution there. Even then, Italian people rescued and protected most Jews.

The Italian government introduced anti-Jewish laws in 1938. Jews could not study or teach in public schools. But the government permitted separate schools. Foreign Jews could not become residents of Italy. That was to keep out the Jews fleeing Germany and Austria at the time. Jews who had moved to Italy after 1919 could not become residents. Still, the Italian laws were a pale imitation of the German laws. Italian officials were lax about carrying out the laws.

The Italians could not persecute the Jews on the basis of their bloodlines, as the Germans did. That's because the Roman

Catholic Church spoke out on behalf of those Jews who converted to Catholicism. Offspring of mixed marriages were given time to convert in order to avoid being defined as Jews.

German family courts traced records doggedly to find out who was Jewish. In Italy bribery was common. People easily counterfeited official Italian documents. Only those Jews who refused to lie about their backgrounds were persecuted.

Italy entered World War II in 1940. Foreign Jews, almost all of whom were fleeing Belgium, the Netherlands, and France, were sent to Italian concentration camps. Italian Jews were placed under a mild form of house arrest.

The camps in Italy were ruled with a gentle hand unheard of in Germany. Prisoners were allowed to set up nurseries, libraries, schools, theaters, and synagogues. They held concerts and athletic competitions. Some camps even had public baths and drug stores.

Italy controlled the areas of Croatia, Greece, and southern France. In those areas, the Italians refused to cooperate with Hitler's Final Solution. Only after Italy pulled out of Greece did the Nazis round up the Jews.

In October 1943, while the people of Denmark were rescuing Danish Jews, the Nazis struck in Italy. The Nazis plundered the offices of the Jewish community in Rome. They took money, historical books, artwork, and most importantly, a list of Roman Jews. Jewish leaders failed to act when warned. They thought the Nazis would not have the nerve to deport Jews from the backyard of the Pope. But in two days, the Nazis had rounded up 12,000 Jews and sent them to Auschwitz.

In Venice, the leader of the Jewish community burned the list of Venetian Jews and committed suicide. Many Jews escaped. In Florence, Rabbi Nathan Cassuto went door to door warning the Jews to hide. Only four hundred Jews were deported from that city.

The Vatican had been told of the deportations but the Pope refused to do anything. The German ambassador wrote: "The Pope, although beseeched by various sides, has not allowed himself to be drawn into any statement against the deportation of the Jews of Rome."

Without waiting for the Pope to speak, hundreds of priests, nuns, bishops, and clerics, aided the Jews. Jews hid in churches, monasteries, and convents.

The ovens of the Nazi death camps where so many
Jewish people perished.

In the fall and winter of 1943 to1944, the government told the Italian police to arrest Jews. Some police warned the Jews ahead of time in order to let them escape.

The Italian Jews were lucky. In Poland the Nazis had five years to do their dirty work. In the Netherlands they had four. In Italy, however, they had only one year. So in spite of the Nazi efforts, eight out of ten Italian Jews escaped death. Eight thousand were murdered in the death camps.

CHAPTER ELEVEN

THE NETHERLANDS

*T*he Netherlands, a small country north of Germany, is sometimes called Holland. People who live in the Netherlands are called Dutch. When the Nazis invaded the Netherlands on May 10, 1940, the Dutch people were shocked. During World War I, the Germans had respected the neutrality of the Dutch. This time, the Germans overran the Netherlands in seven days. Rotterdam was bombed mercilessly, leaving much of the city in ruins.

Unlike other countries, the Nazis ruled the Netherlands with both military and civil control. The Nazis appointed five German generals to oversee the five branches of the Dutch government. The same Nazi commissioner who had ruled over Austria's succession to Germany in 1938 was appointed to rule the Netherlands.

The Nazis respected the Dutch. The Nazis thought of them as perfect Aryans—part of Hitler's master race. Hitler considered the Dutch to be a Germanic tribe and demanded that they join the Nazi cause. Because of this, the Nazis applied their racial laws more strictly in the Netherlands than they had elsewhere. Dutch Jews were made to suffer in an even more mean-spirited way than their cousins in Belgium and France.

In 1940 the Netherlands counted 140,000 Jews. They had been drawn to that small country by its traditions of art, education, and tolerance. Jews were completely accepted as equals by most Dutch people.

Once the Nazi government was in place in the Netherlands, however, anti-Jewish laws were quickly enacted. Protests erupted at universities in which a large percent of students and teachers were involve. Nonetheless, all Jewish professors were fired. Protests again erupted. The Nazis soon realized that it would take a long time to bring the Netherlands into the Nazi fold.

Since the occupation of the Netherlands occurred at beginning of the Final Solution, no one knew what to expect. When the Nazis demanded that all Jews register with the government, most did. When the Nazis sent the Jews to the death camps, the Dutch thought that the Jews were only going to labor camps. Many Jews figured they could survive better there than in life on the run. They didn't know they would be killed upon arrival.

In 1941 violence erupted in the Jewish quarter in the Dutch city of Amsterdam. Jews were defending themselves against Nazi attack. The Nazis rounded up 425 Jewish youths at random. The Nazis brutally beat the youths and sent them to death camps. This incident shook the Dutch awake.

Strikes broke out all over the country. Shipyards and metalworks were shut down. This was the first public protest against the Nazis anywhere in Europe. The Nazis arrested and beat many of the ringleaders.

In July 1942, the Nazis packed 95,000 Dutch Jews into cattle cars and sent them to death camps in faraway Poland. The long, tortuous train ride killed thousands. Of the 95,000 sent to the camps, only 1,100 survived. Of the 34,000 sent to Sobibor camp, only 19 survived. Twenty-five thousand Jews went into hiding. Of those, about 8,500 were eventually discovered and sent to their deaths. In all, eight out of ten Dutch Jews died in the camps.

German women remove death camp victims for burial.

But the Dutch made the best of a horrible situation. Police officers resigned from their jobs rather than arrest Jews. Churches urged their members to protest the Nazis with actions rather than words. The Dutch underground moved Jews from one hiding place to another. They distributed food stamps and rations to families who housed Jews.

Some people were forced to move dozens of times. Some people hid Jews in exchange for large sums of money. Soon the Nazis had to offer rewards for Jews in hiding. Those caught hiding the Jews were sent to the camps.

CHAPTER TWELVE

ANNE FRANK

*T*he most well-known account of a Jew in hiding is the Anne Frank story.

Otto and Edith Frank escaped Nazi Germany in the mid-1930s with their daughters, Margot and Anne. In 1941 when the Nazis demanded that all Jewish businesses be sold, Otto transferred the two firms he owned to his trusted associates, Jan Kleinman and Victor Kugler.

The Franks soon realized that they would have to go into hiding. They furnished and equipped two upper floors of a building with the help of Kugler, Kleinman, and Miep Gies and Elisabeth Van Voskuijl. These two floors were separated from the rest of the building by a staircase. A false bookcase hid the staircase.

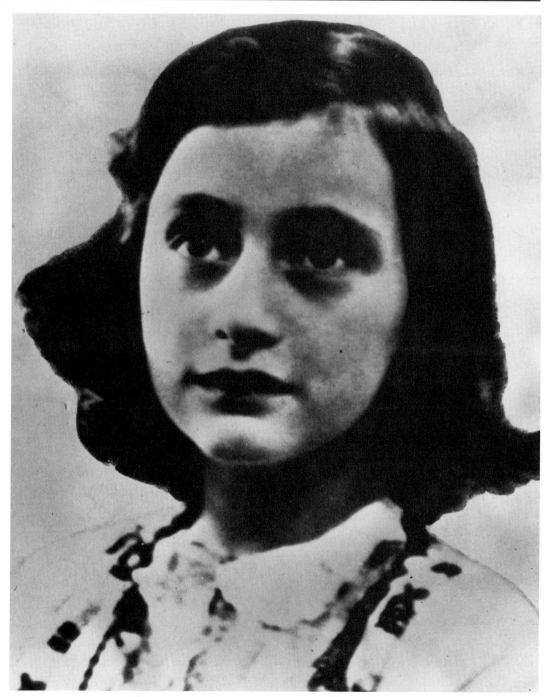

Anne Frank, Nazi victim.

On July 5, 1942, Margot received notice to report to a transport camp. The next morning, the Franks moved into the hidden rooms together with another family, the Van Daans. To give the impression that they had left the country, a friend posted a farewell letter written by Otto Frank.

For the next two years, the Franks and the Van Daans never left their hidden rooms. They were joined later by an elderly dentist named Albert Dussel.

The eight prisoners of the upstairs hideout were totally dependent on their four Dutch friends for food and news. Sometimes the friends made up good news to lift the Frank's spirits. The families eagerly sought magazines and newspapers to relieve boredom. Anne even enrolled in a Latin class by mail.

On August 4, 1944, an informer betrayed the family. Police raided the hideout. The eight Jews were taken to Auschwitz. Except for Otto, none of them survived. Anne died of typhus on a death march a few weeks before the war ended.

The Nazis sent Kugler and Kleinman to a Dutch concentration camp. Kleinman was released with the help of the Red Cross. Kugler did seven months of hard labor then escaped. He hid with relatives until the end of the war. Kugler moved to Canada in 1948. When asked years later about hiding the Franks, he said, "I tried to save the lives of my friends. And it is my greatest sorrow that I failed. What else could I have done?.... I don't understand what the fuss is about."

You can read about the hardships that the Franks suffered in *The Diary of Anne Frank*. This story of a teenage girl with hopes and dreams, surviving under horrid conditions, is a moving one.

When the Nazis arrested Anne Frank, Anne's diary was thrown on the floor. A neighbor saved it and Otto Frank had it published after the war. Today, *The Diary of Anne Frank* has sold more than twenty million copies in dozens of languages. It has also been turned into a Broadway play and a major motion picture.

Mr. Otto Frank, father of Anne Frank, shows Queen Juliana of the Netherlands the hiding place of the Frank family during World War II. In 1979, the Queen visited the Anne Frank house in Amsterdam on Anne Frank's 50th birthday anniversary.

CHAPTER THIRTEEN

RESISTANCE IN GERMANY

*G*ermany was the home of the Nazis. When Adolf Hitler came to power in January 30, 1933, anti-Jewish laws were passed quickly. The Nazis removed Jews from professions including law, culture, media, and public health. They removed Jews from schools. By 1938 the Nazis forcibly removed Jews from their homes and transferred them to overcrowded "Jewish houses." They took businesses from their Jewish owners. They barred Jews from country clubs and resorts. The Nazis did not allow Jews to own a telephone or an automobile. In 1942 German Jews were forced to wear a large yellow, six-pointed Star of David sewn to their clothing. This made rounding them up easier.

In 1933 the German Jewish population was about 500,000. When the Nazis took over Austria, that added another 200,000 Jews. By 1942 most of the Jews had left Germany for other countries. About 260,000 Jews remained. Of those, 90 percent were murdered. Most of the others were rounded up and killed in the countries where they had fled.

Germany was without a doubt the most dangerous country in which to defy the Nazis. Their spies were everywhere.

But even in the heart of Nazism there was resistance. Some of the opposition to Hitler came from wealthy aristocrats. They viewed Hitler as a crude commoner. They were appalled that he had turned their country into a police state. A small group of these people put their lives on the line to stop Hitler.

For years a group within the German officer corps plotted to kill Hitler and seize power. The officers made a serious assassination attempt in July 1944. They exploded a bomb. Amazingly, Hitler escaped serious injuries. Dozens of officers were hung for their part in the plot.

A few young people in Germany organized a movement called White Rose. They held public demonstrations

Arrest of Jewish people by Nazis after the Warsaw ghetto insurrection.

against the Nazis. At the head of White Rose was a medical student named Christoph Probst and his sister Sophie. They were outraged at the treatment of the Jews and Poles.

The group handed out leaflets and letters urging people to resist. But the Nazis rounded up leaders of the movement and executed them.

Still, in all the madness, thousands of Germans in all walks of life hid Jews. Some three thousand Jews managed to survive the war in Berlin.

CHAPTER FOURTEEN

OSKAR SCHINDLER

*T*oday, Oskar Schindler has found a new fame, thanks to filmmaker Steven Spielberg. In 1993 Spielberg directed *Schindler's List*, a movie of one man's stand against the Nazis.

Schindler was an ethnic German born in Moravia, which today is in Czechoslovakia. Schindler's country was annexed by the Nazis in 1938.

Towards the end of 1939, Schindler took over an enamelware factory in Cracow, Poland. The factory made pots and pans for the German Army. Jews had owned the factory until the Nazis took it over. Before long, the factory had 900 workers, most of them Jews.

In April 1943 the Nazis emptied the Cracow ghetto. The 6,000 Jews there were sent to a labor camp at nearby Plaszów. Schindler persuaded the Nazis to let him set up a branch camp on the factory grounds. This way, the workers would not have to go back and forth to the camp. Schindler's real purpose was to protect the Jews from the terrible conditions at the concentration camp.

By 1944 the Red (Soviet) Army had moved into Poland. Again Schindler confronted Nazi authorities. This time he persuaded them to move his now-closed enamel plant to a Moravian town. This plant, said Schindler, would make bullets and bombs. He also wanted to take his entire group of workers.

The Nazis allowed Schindler to take 1,100 Jews with him. This was an event entirely unique in the history of the Holocaust. Many of Schindler's workers were too old, sick, or weak to actually work, but they were saved. As with his old factory, Schindler treated the Jews well. He found them food, clothing, and medicine.

Later in the winter, Schindler found out that the Nazis had abandoned a train full of Jews in a nearby town. They had left their human cargo to die in the bitter cold. Schindler and several workers found the train and broke open the locks on the ice-covered boxcars. Schindler rescued the 100 men and women left alive. With his wife, Emilie, the survivors were nursed back to health. Those who died were buried with traditional Jewish rites.

One survivor of Schindler's factory wrote: "He was the first German since the beginning of the war whose presence did not terrify me."

After the war Schindler admitted he only went to Poland to get rich. He hoped to exploit the slave labor there. At the beginning, he seemed no different than the other German masters. But as the war went on, his personality changed. In the end, though arrested several times by the Gestapo, Schindler remained true to the compassion in his heart.

Schindler was shocked by the Final Solution. He said:

> I hated the brutality, the sadism, and the insanity of Nazism. I just couldn't stand by and see people destroyed. I did what I could, what I had to do, what my conscience told me I must do. That's all there is to it. Really, nothing more.

In the end, 1,200 Jews owed their lives to Oskar Schindler. Today, the descendants of "Schindler's Jews" number 6,000.

In 1980 author Thomas Keneally was shopping in a store in Beverly Hills when the owner began to tell him the story of Oskar Schindler. The store's owner, Leopold Page, was one of "Schindler's Jews." For thirty years, Page had been telling every writer, director, and movie producer he met about Schindler. By 1982, the story of Oskar Schindler had been written in a prize-winning book by Keneally.

Oskar Schindler with many of the Schindler Jews in Israel.

In 1993 award-winning director Steven Spielberg turned Keneally's book into a movie, *Schindler's List*. The three-hour movie brought the frightening reality of the Holocaust to life for a new generation. Spielberg shot the film in Poland and visited the old haunts where the events took place—Schindler's factory is still standing.

When *Schindler's List* was released it broke records for movie attendance. It won seven Academy Awards, including best picture, best director, and best adapted screenplay. One day after the movie won the Academy Awards, over 100,000 people went to see it. When the movie was shown in Germany and Poland, it was well received. In several countries, plans to ban the film or censor several scenes were overturned by public pressure.

What ever happened to Schindler? He moved to Argentina in 1949. After failing in business there, he abandoned his wife and went back to Germany. There, he ran several businesses into the ground and became an alcoholic. In 1961 Schindler traveled to Israel where he lived with several "Schindler's Jews." He died in Frankfurt in 1974 at the age of 66.

Some survivors are not happy with the efforts to make Schindler look like a saint. One said: "We owe our lives to him. But I wouldn't glorify a German because of what he did to us. There is no proportion."

But the heroic efforts of Oskar Schindler have been honored with a plaque in the Park of Heroes in Tel Aviv, Israel. The city of Yad Vashem declared him a "righteous person" and honored him with a tree on that city's Avenue of the Righteous. Today, Schindler's grave is a tourist attraction in Israel.

CHAPTER FIFTEEN

REFUGE IN THE KILLING GROUNDS OF POLAND

*W*hen the Nazis invaded Poland on September 1, 1939, World War II began. The people in Poland had no idea what the Nazis had in store for them. Hitler's grand plan was to kill everybody in Poland, destroy its cities, and move Germans onto the land. The Poles that remained would be slaves to their master Nazis. Hitler planned to "Germanize" Poland completely in twenty-five to thirty years. The country slated for destruction by the Nazis also happened to contain 3,250,000 Jews. This was the largest concentration of Jews in Europe.

Because of Hitler's master plan, no mercy was to be shown to Poland. A reign of terror was started that was unbelievably cruel—even by Nazi standards. The entire country was to be treated like a concentration camp. The only people allowed freedom of movement would be the guards. All Polish children with Aryan features were removed to Germany to be "Germanized." Some 250,000 children were kidnapped for this purpose. Universities and schools were closed. Massive arrests and street sweeps yielded slave labor for concentration camps. Germans were legally allowed to shoot Poles for whatever reason they chose.

Except for the Jews, the Poles suffered more cruelty at Nazi hands than any other people. Yet a wide gulf existed between the Poles and the Polish Jews. The Jews spoke their own language, Yiddish. They stood out from the Poles in dress, habits, names, and manner. Though they had been in Poland for nine hundred years, they were not considered equals in Polish society. Respected historians have said that even before the war, Poland was the most anti-Jewish country in Europe, after Nazi Germany.

When the Nazis tried to implement the Final Solution, many Poles eagerly helped. Poles often led Nazis to Jewish apartments, then looted and took over the property. Polish children hunted Jews for sport. Most Polish Jews were more afraid of the Poles than they were of the Nazis. In fact the Polish word for Jew is considered a racist curse. Sensitive or educated Poles prefer the words "Hebrew" or "Israelite" when describing Jewish people.

The Polish Jews were the poorest Jews in all of Europe and had very little power. The Polish government had actually tried to get the League of Nations (the 1920s version of the United Nations) to give Poland distant colonies that it could ship its Jews to. Thus, the general wish of most Poles was that it wanted its country cleansed of Jews. The Nazis would be only too happy to make that a reality.

In 1940 the Nazis began moving Jews from all over Poland into Warsaw. More than 500,000 were herded into a tiny part of town. Barbed wire fences and armed guards kept the Jews confined to the ghetto. Other ghettos were set up in other cities such as Lodz and Cracow. Tens of thousands of Jews died of starvation and disease in the ghettos.

A few years later, Poland became the main killing ground for the slaughter of Europe's Jews. The Polish countryside became dotted with death camps whose names (Treblinka, Chelmno, Auschwitz, Belzec, Majdanek) have left permanent stains on the human record. There, the practice of mass murder was elevated to scientific perfection. More than four million Jews saw the last light of day on Polish soil. The vast number of men, women, and children who were Poland's Jews were also trapped in this mass inferno.

All this took place in full view of the local populations. Local people could not help but hear the cries of the doomed as the trains inched towards the camps. Nor could they miss the smoke that belched from the crematoria furnaces.

How could the Poles react to this situation? The Jews were physically trapped. There were no escape routes. The Nazis occupied every country surrounding Poland. Inside Poland, there was a dizzying array of German military and security forces. No other country had as many Germans occupying it. And the weight of the evidence suggests that most Poles were glad to be rid of the 10 percent of their population that was Jewish. All the blame for this deed would fall directly on German shoulders.

Poland had the largest underground Nazi-resistance movement of any country. Broad masses of men—as many as 380,000—signed up with secret armies to fight the Nazis. But even the underground refused to help the Jews in their midst. Some resistance armies actually organized mass killings of Jews. In fact fiercely anti-Jewish armies continued to mass-murder Jews *after* the war and after the Nazis had left. Today, there is almost nothing left of the centuries-old Polish Jewish community, once the largest in the world.

Under these horrible conditions, almost any Jew who survived the Holocaust in Poland was helped by a non-Jew. And the Nazis made it clear that helping Jews was punishable by death. They posted notices on bulletin boards and in newspapers warning

Poles to ignore the Jewish plight. Some Poles who helped Jews were hung by the neck from the balconies of their apartments as a warning to others. Others had their farms burned to the ground. In addition, a Pole could be murdered for simply selling food to a Jew or giving them a ride in their vehicle. In no other country was aiding the Jews punished with such severe treatment as in Poland.

Jewish people being sent to the ghettos in Warsaw, Poland.

The threat to the rescuers came not only from the Nazis but from neighbors and even their relatives. There are stories of rescuers being turned in by their own family members who were mad that the rescuer would help the "despised" Jew. Many rescuers suffered violence *after* the war when their brave deeds of rescue became known. Some had to leave their towns to escape violence from their own people. Thus Polish rescuers faced double jeopardy for their humanitarian acts. Nearly forty Polish rescuers live in Israel today, some with or near the people they saved.

At one time Poland was the cultural, scientific, and religious center for more than three million Jewish people. Only 6,000 Jews remain in Poland today.

CHAPTER SIXTEEN

IN THEIR OWN WORDS

*O*f the nine million Jews living in Europe in 1933, six million were murdered. Of the three million who survived, many owe their lives to non-Jewish rescuers. These men and women protected the hunted Jews with their lives. They unlocked doors. They built secret rooms. They hid Jews in cellars, sewers, and barnyards. They stole food. They lied to the killers. They forged passports, visas, and baptismal certificates in the face of death. They treated the wounded, fed the hungry, and buried the dead.

Jews do not believe that a human can ever see the face of God. But some Jews believe that they can see God's goodness in the faces of the rescuers.

It has been fifty years since the killing stopped. Age has not been kind to many of the rescuers. Some are needy, hungry, and ill. Some have moved to Israel. They are dependent on those who once depended on them.

There have been and will be millions of words written to describe the Holocaust. Many will describe the evil. Some will describe the good. But nothing could better describe the rescuers than their own words. Here are a few words from the many thousands who cared when many millions did not.

> *God gives us life as a precious loan. No one but God has the right to reclaim it. That's all I know. The rest is unimportant.* —Eduard Fajks, Poland

What I did for the Jewish people... was but a [small] contribution...to prevent this horrible slaughter, unprecedented and satanic, of more than six million Jews. [This] will remain the foulest stain in all of human history, a shame affecting all who participated or allowed it to happen. —Father Marc-Benoit, France

I did nothing but put into practice the values of Christianity and of love of one's fellow man.
—Edouard Vigneron, France

I did nothing special and I don't consider myself a hero. I simply acted on my human obligation to the persecuted and suffering. I want to emphasize that it was not I who saved them. They saved themselves. I simply gave them a helping hand. I sought no [money] for what I did... and in a way I am proud that while I was once rich, I am now [poor]. To sum up, I should like to say that I did no more than help forty-nine Jews to survive the Holocaust. That's all!
—Wladyslaw Kowalski, Poland

What I did came naturally. It would have been unnatural not to do it.
—Herta Muller-Kuhlenthal, Netherlands

No law in the world says that I should live and you should die. The Nazis have decided that, but I am fighting against them and am not bound by their rules.
—Stanislaw Ogrodzinska, Poland

I ask you (the rescued Jews) *to remain with us for my sake, not yours. If you leave, I shall forever be ashamed to be a member of the human race.*
—Dr. Giovanni Pesante, Italy

GLOSSARY

Allies - the United States, the Soviet Union, Great Britain, France, Canada, and the other countries that came together to fight Germany, Italy, and Japan in World War II.

Anti-Semitism - hatred of Jews.

Aryan - people of Northern European descent.

Concentration camp - a guarded camp for the detention and forced labor of political prisoners.

Cremate, crematoria - to cremate is to burn a dead body; this is done in a crematorium; more than one crematorium are crematoria.

Deportation - to expel from a city, region, or country

Evacuate - to remove for reasons of safety.

Exterminate - to destroy totally.

Gestapo - the German state secret police.

Ghetto - a section of a city in most European countries where all Jews were forced to live.

Holocaust - the mass extermination of Jews in Nazi Germany.

Refugee - a person who flees to a foreign country during a war hoping to find peace or refuge.

Semite - a member of any of a various ancient and modern people, especially Hebrews or Arabs.

Tolerance - a spirit of acceptance to persons, ideas, or practices that differ from one's own.

BIBLIOGRAPHY

Adler, David A. *We Remember the Holocaust.* New York: Henry Holt and Company, 1989.

Aharoni, Yohanan, and Avi-Yonah, Michael. *The Macmillan Bible Atlas.* New York: Macmillan, 1993.

Ausubel, Nathan, and Gross, David C. *Pictorial History of the Jewish People.* New York: Crown Publishers, Inc., 1953, 1984.

Berenbaum, Michael. *The World Must Know.* Boston: Little, Brown and Company, 1993.

Block, Gay, and Drucker. *Malka Rescuers.* New York: Holmes & Meier Publications, Inc., 1992

Chaikin, Miriam A. *Nightmare in History: The Holocaust 1933-1945.* New York: Clarion Books, 1987.

Dawidowicz, Lucy S. *The War Against the Jews 1933-1945.* New York: Seth Press, 1986.

Flannery, Edward H. *The Anguish of the Jews.* New York: Paulist Press, 1985.

Gilbert, Martin. *Final Journey.* New York: Mayflower Books, 1979.

Gilbert, Martin. *The Macmillan Atlas of the Holocaust.* New York: Macmillan, 1982.

Greenfeld, Howard. *The Hidden Children.* New York: Ticknor & Fields, 1993.

Landau, Elaine. *The Warsaw Ghetto Uprising.* New York: New Discovery Books, 1992.

Paldiel, Mordecai. *The Path of the Righteous.* Hoboken, New Jersey: KTAV Publishing House, Inc., 1993.

Index